Simply Speaking with God

Inspirational Poetry

J. Michael

iUniverse, Inc.
New York Bloomington

Simply Speaking with God
Inspirational Poetry

iUniverse books may be ordered through booksellers or by contacting:

iUniverse
1663 Liberty Drive
Bloomington, IN 47403
www.iuniverse.com
1-800-Authors (1-800-288-4677)

Because of the dynamic nature of the Internet, any Web addresses or links contained in this book may have changed since publication and may no longer be valid.

ISBN: 978-1-4502-7203-2 (sc)
ISBN: 978-1-4502-7204-9 (dj)
ISBN: 978-1-4502-7205-6 (ebk)

Library of Congress Control Number: 2010917276

Printed in the United States of America

iUniverse rev. date: 11/23/2010

Acknowledgements

This book of poetry is a "must read" whether you are an avid reader of poetry or not. You will find this book inspiring and each poem will touch your heart in a different way.

Carl Easterling
Electrical Consultants Project Manager

Reading J. Michael's poetry was like waking up to a new life. The memories of family and friends all came rushing back. The daily devotionals will be a continuing part of my life. This is a "must read book". It will change your life.

Katrina Mabry Davis
Business Owner

For the young and old alike. I hope that you will take the opportunity to read these heartfelt words. After reading J. Michael's poems, I feel there is indeed a light at the end of the tunnel where my Redeemer waits for me." I am truly inspired.

Mary Mauldin Lee
Professional Secretary

J Michael truly has a God given talent. The writing of this poetry, no doubt, will bring glory and honor to our Lord and Savior. I believe this collection to be J. Michael's genuine heart and soul. This poetry will bless you in ways you can not imagine.

Cecilia Diggs Carter

Contents

Chapter 1   *Prayer Poems* *1*
My Special Day 2
A Cry For Help 4
Your Kingdom 6
Bless My Friends 8
The Dying Of A Saint 10
Your Birthday 12
A Request and Answer 14
My True and Living God 16
Say Hello 18
While We Were Yet Sinners (Romans 5:8) 20
The Garden 22
Guard My Mind 24
Love Me Dear Lord 26
At This Time For Rest 28
Jesus, My Special Friend 30
Blessings For My Home 32
I Shall Rejoice 34
God's Helpers 36

Chapter 2   *Special Poems* *39*
My Darling Lori 40
The Wall (Dedication Poem) 42
The Preacher Man 44
The Day Grandpa Went Away 46
The Waterfall 48
Far Over Daytona Beach 49
The Warriors 50
A Dream Come True 52
Happiness 54
He Lives 56
God and Butterflies 57
Where Are You Lord 58
The Places I Would Love To Bring You 60
That Special Sunday 62
Precious In The Eyes Of The Lord (Psalm 116:15) 64
Not For Sale 66

Father's Day 68
What A Blessing You Are 70
Honest To The Core 72
Music From The Air 74
My Patio 76
What Will You Do 78
Beyond Tampa Bay 80
Love Flows Like A River. 82
The Gathering 83
The Day We All Come Back Together 84
The Love of A Woman 86
My Home Town. 88

Chapter 3   Devotional Poems **89**
The Creator 90
GO (Matt 28:19-20) 96
A Place Called Calvary (Mark 15:37). 98
The Changed Man (Mark 9:2-10) 100
The Harvest (Matt 9: 35-38) 102
The Model From The Model (Matt 6:9-13) 104
God's Lamb (various). 106
Never Doubt (Matt 14:22-33) 108
The Promises (Matt 5:3-11) 112
Happy Will Be My Days 114
The 5 K (Matthew 14:1- 21) 118
Why Do We Worship The Lord (various). 120
To Honor The Lord (Psalm 23) 122
What Is The Word (various). 123
The Forgiver (Various) 124
He Speaks (Matt 7:21-24a) 128
Paul Said (Various). 130
Seven Last Comments (various) 131
He Arrives (Matthew 3) 132
My Daily Blessings. 134
His Love (Ephesians 3:15) 138
Faith (Hebrews 11) 140
My Hope For You 142

Introduction

This book of poems is a testimony from me to my Almighty God. These poems are in ode form, and each tells a story and are very easily read. This is my way to show all generations just how easy it is to talk to our Heavenly Father.

These poems are rhetoric of military service, work, travel, service to God, my life, amongst other experiences.

The poems are in the form of Special Poems, Prayer Poems, and Devotional Poems.

I give the credit to God for touching me in all the ways that he has.

He is an awesome God.

These poems tell of things lost and things found, things old and things new.

Many of you will relate to some of these small tokens from my heart. My prayer is that, as you read you will allow God to touch you in that very special way.

May God Bless You

J. Michael

About The Author

J. Michael was born in NC in 1950 and is the eldest son of three. He is a high school graduate and a Vietnam Veteran. He married in 1972 and his daughter was born in 1975. 10 months later, she went home to be with Jesus.

For over 30 years, J. Michael predominately worked in the Nuclear Power Industry, served as a Missionary, and was also a licensed Minister and was used as a Supply Pastor.

In 2006, his 35 year marriage came to an end.

J. Michael struggled for a time trying to find a way of life that would give him purpose once again. Writing Spiritual Poetry was his therapy and he continues to enjoy it to this day.

He enjoys researching and verifying the intent of Scripture and often uses the works of Rev. Charles Spurgeon.

Charles Spurgeon wrote the following quote during the late 1800s that J. Michael loves to read and shares frequently. He has chosen to share this quote with you.

> *Now, dear friends, as the tests are so severe, you see how it is that the righteous are only saved with difficulty. Oh, if I may but come out of that scale full weight, if I may but come out of that fire as pure gold, if I may but remain with the wheat in that sieve, and not be blown away with the chaff, I shall bless God for ever and ever that I was saved, even though it was with great difficulty.*
>
> *Further, the experience of all Christians proves that the work of grace in their hearts is not easily accomplished, said that their pilgrimage to heaven is full of difficulties.*

At the very beginning of the Christian life some find it hard to lay hold on Christ. We truly sing or say:

"There is life for a look at the Crucified One.

Yet there was a time when I felt that I would gladly give my life in exchange for that look.

Easy as it seems to be to cast ourselves into the Savior's arms there are satanic doubts, and evil questionings, and fierce temptations that cause even that simple act to be accomplished only with great difficulty. Indeed, wherever it is accomplished it is a miracle of divine mercy, in every case saving faith is "the gift of God."

Today, J. Michael lives back in North Carolina where he is active in the Church and is forever writing for and praising his beloved Lord.

Dedication

To all of those brave men and women who have served, are serving now, and will serve in the future in the uniform of the United States of America.

I also dedicate to the memory of all those who have fallen in battle for the preservation of freedom.

Psalm 45:1 My heart is moved by a noble theme: as I speak my verses to the king: my tongue is the pen of a skillful writer.

Chapter 1

Prayer Poems

My Special Day

Thank you Father for touching me,
In Your very special way.
You allow me to see Your presence,
Each and every day.

I know You are in everything,
That I see and that I feel.
You give me all I need,
To do Your precious will.

A lot of times I fail,
But I know You love me still.
You promised us eternal life,
And Your blood was the seal.

Every day You give me the vision,
To see the things You have done.
Everything is so connected,
To the glory of Your Son.

I pray dear Father,
That something I may say or that I may do,
Will lead some lost soul,
To bring their heart to you.

Where would I be Lord,
If You were not there on that special day.
I would be lost Lord,
I would have never found my way.

To stay on that wide road,
Oh how sad that would be!
To be in the darkness looking,
But never a light to see.

Some think the narrow road costs too much,
But it is totally free.
I remember so very well,
How free it was for me.

You ask me to come to You,
And trust in Your call.
You said I have a special gift for you,
For it is the greatest gift of all.

The gift was the best,
And now I understand that You are the only way.
For You took my sins and saved my soul,
On this my special day.

A Cry For Help

This morning as I come to You,
Oh my precious Father.
My soul is troubled Lord,
And You I don't want to bother.

But I need You to hear me Lord,
And help me if You can.
I need to feel Your precious touch,
And help this sinful man.

I feel so alone my Lord;
I have only You to talk to.
I love to be near you Father,
All the long day through.

You said that You would never leave me,
I believe this is true.
My soul is crying for help Lord,
It's You I bring it to.

Have I in some awful way
Walked away from You,.
Lord I humbly repent,
If what I say is true.

I feel so empty Lord
At times my spirit seems so weak.
I try to keep You in my mind,
For Your will is what I seek.

My purpose in life Lord,
Seems to be all but gone.
Have I thrown it away Lord?
Is this why I'm all alone?

Father I will talk to You,
All day if you would hear the words I say.
I know that You love me Lord,
For it's in Jesus' name I pray.

Your Kingdom

As I sat late last night,
Looking up to Thee,
You filled my soul with happiness,
Your throne I could almost see.

And as I saw all the stars,
That are so greatly Thine,
I know that all Your victories,
Are also those of mine.

They appeared to form a stairway,
That I know will lead to You.
They adorn Your beautiful heaven,
And all You created too.

I use to view them as far out of reach,
For I can't see them in the day.
But You made me realize late last night,
They are not that far away.

You have created a wonderful universe,
With lights that please the eye.
You made them oh so beautiful,
And placed them in the sky.

When we talk to each other,
As Father and as son,
I can hear Your loving voice ,
Explaining all that You have done.

So as we grow closer to Thee,
Will you fix in our mind,
That we can have here on earth,
A heaven so loving and kind?

So we want to thank You Lord,
For The love You placed within our soul.
For it is all so very true,
Just as Jesus has told.

In this world some day,
We shall all harmoniously live.
And praises of honor and glory,
We shall to Thee so humbly give.

Bless My Friends

I need to thank you Lord,
For these special friends of mine.
They have been so good to me,
Friends like this are hard to find.

I remember that Jesus said,
I have no place to lay My head.
They offered me a place Lord,
And a warm comfortable bed.

When all the rest of my so-called friends,
To me did turn their back,.
My real friends showed Your love to me,
Nothing did they lack.

They love me Lord like family,
And I know that it comes from You.
Without my special friends Lord,
I would not know what to do.

They offered me some land Lord,
So close by them I could live.
It was a gift from their hearts Lord,
Freely they would give

They called me all the time Lord,
Just to see if I am doing fine.
They are my earthly rocks Lord,
They are so loving and kind.

Would you bless them Lord,
For they love you oh so much.
Would you expand their coast Lord?
And let them feel your tender touch.?

I miss them Lord when I am away,
But I hope to see them real soon.
They have brought me out of midnight Lord,
To see Your blessed noon.

He sings Your praises Lord,
To all that he can.
He is a solid witness for You,
This very godly man.

We worshiped You together Lord,
Those days I won't forget.
To preach Your blessed word Lord,
I never will regret

Bless his wife Lord, for her support,
Which I have so richly gained.
Would you heal her Lord,
And give her comfort from her pain.

She is Your servant to Lord,
Your praises she does say.
Would You bless my loving friends Lord,
In every single way?

The Dying Of A Saint

Oh Lord,
Your attention this moment may I seize?
One of Your servants is dying,
Of a terrible disease.

He is Your anointed,
And Your word he did teach.
You are the one he loved, obeyed,
And did so boldly preach.

Would You touch him this day,
And Your love let him feel.
For his life was rich in You,
And his love is oh so real.

He loved Your creations,
His family and all that You blessed.
Would You this day give him peace,
And give him peaceful rest?

You have set his time,
To come home to You.
His work on earth is finished,
It Is finally through.

His presence here on earth,
We will surely miss.
Because his passion for You,
Was one of spiritual bliss.

When he arrives in Your presence,
Crowns You will give.
For the work he did,
And the life he did live.

I know that on that day Your angels,
Will sing a special cord.
Well done good and faithful servant,
Enter into the kingdom of thy Lord.

Your Birthday

Fall is in the air,
And I feel so special this time of year.
My thoughts of you are heavenly,
And my soul is full of cheer.

I feel that we should realize,
The importance of this day.
I feel we should be grateful for it,
In a very special way.

Because I know You personally,
Your love to others I shall speak.
Your love has made us all stronger,
And has never made us weak.

You were born in a special way back then;
It was very timely and so bold.
Because of Your love and kindness,
You have brought many to Your fold.

May everyone help me celebrate Your birth,
To the fullness of You, my friend.
Help me to teach that all year long,
That this party should never end.

To the glory of You we should celebrate,
And to be more like You, we should strive.
And to thank You for Your gift to us,
And be grateful You did arrive.

I love to celebrate Your birthday,
And am as happy as I can be.
May I smile as I prepare for it,
And hope the whole world will see.

Soon we shall celebrate together,
And I will have the honor to say,
I am glad to be with You Lord,
To celebrate this Christmas day.

A Request and Answer

Please guard us Father,
When dangers shall assail.
And teach us that Thy power,
Can never, ever fail.

I face trials in my heart,
That sometime seem to stay.
I need You Lord,
Can You help me chase them away.

I trust in my Lord Jesus,
To never let me fall.
I am trusting in Him forever,
For I love Him most of all.

Our Father said every joy, or trial,
Falleth from above.
Traced upon your life,
By the Son of love.

You must trust me wholly,
And that's what you must do.
If you trust me wholly,
You will find me holy true.

Midst green pastures,
I will lead my sheep where living streams appear.
And Jesus my Son from every eye,
Shall wipe away every tear.

He is the way, the truth, and the life,
And He will grant you this way to know.
That truth to keep, that life to win,
Whose joys eternally flow.

You cannot tell what gladness,
May be yours today.
What sorrow or temptation,
May meet you along your way.

This you know most surely,
That through all good or ill,
That the grace of Jesus Christ,
Can help you do My will.

My True and Living God

Father I know that You come to us daily,
In all the things we see.
For all things You created,
We are forever grateful to Thee.

To watch the sun rise,
That gloriously adorns the day,
It is so beautiful to see,
Every inch of the way.

Early in the morning,
As I watch for this to start,
I know You are looking down on me,
And we shall never part.

Today You'll look at all You have made,
With love as Your thought.
Freely You gave it all to us,
And nothing had to be bought.

Teach me to rejoice,
As together we start a brand new time.
Help me to understand,
That Your love is also that of mine.

As I travel throughout this life,
Let something I say or do,
Help someone understand,
The love and the glory of You.

Will You this day bless us,
To the extent of Your will.
And help us all to understand,
That on our hearts You put a seal.

To your own honor and glory,
You give us a way to choose.
To commit to your eternal teachings,
We can never ever lose.

To talk to You daily,
I shall never want to nod.
Continuously I want to thank You,
for being my true and living God.

Say Hello

As I slowly open my eyes,
And stretch in every way,
I found that God has given me,
Yet another day.

And as I stumble up,
From the comfort of my bed,
A wonderful and happy thought,
Filled my sleepy head.

Should I go to work,
Or out to play today?
So I thought to ask God,
To see what He would say.

I said to the Father,
Which will it be this beautiful new morn?
It is so wonderfully bright,
Like the day Jesus was born.

Shall it be toil or folly?
I asked Him up above.
He said which ever you choose my child,
Only do it with love.

It is sometimes hard to work,
On the day you wish to play.
But with the love of Christ in your heart,
You can do them both today.

I gave you my beloved Son,
So you could be happy in this way.
Do everything with His love,
That He promised would never go away.

When you rise each morning,
And there's something you wish to know,
Ask Me I will tell you straight,
For I love it when you say hello.

While We Were Yet Sinners
(Romans 5:8)

Dear Jesus you were there,
When we thought we were all alone.
You came to show us a light,
That would lead us to our home.

Our father planted you in Mary,
Who would be your Blessed Mother.
You were a gift from Him to us,
Because there could be no other.

You are the Christ,
Of which the prophets did bravely speak.
You are the way of life,
That we all should humbly seek.

I am so glad You came,
For our Father's kingdom you did teach.
Then You sent us Paul,
To show us how we should preach.

Thank You for the blood,
Which You shed on Calvary's hill.
Through Your obedience,
You mastered the Father's will.

You alone won the victory,
Over death and the grave.
You made us heirs to Your kingdom,
Through the life that You gave.

Thank You for loving us,
And making us more than winners.
For we know You died for us all,
While we were yet sinners.

The Garden

Being in the garden early,
Gives me pleasure that never goes away.
I love to watch the butterflies,
As they float around and play.

To watch sandpipers,
As they come out and start their day,
There are things we can learn from them,
I think that You would say.

How beautiful is the sunrise!
And see the flowers start to unfold.
These are just a few things You do,
That go so untold.

Many will not give you the credit,
For all these things they see.
Some think things just happen,
They don't think they come from Thee.

I feel the closest to You,
When I come to the garden alone.
I walk with You and talk with You,
And you tell me I am your own.

Your voice is dear as I hear,
What Your words clearly disclose.
Your voice is so much sweeter,
Than the scent of Your beautiful rose.

Being in the garden is a special place for me,
Every single day.
I see Your touch in everything,
And I see it in a very special way.

Thank You for the blessings You give to me,
As through the garden we walk.
Thank You for giving me the garden,
So that You and I may talk.

Guard My Mind

As I lay down at this night and time,
I ask Thee oh God for a smile to find.
And as I sleep so softly and sweet,
I ask that You guard my mind.

Keep bad and evil dreams away,
Keep them from entering my head.
And let me dream sweet dreams of You,
And Your sweet love instead.

I love to rest,
In Your arms at night.
Knowing that You,
Will hold me tight.

Hold me close o' Lord;
Hold me with all Your might.
O hold me close o' Lord,
And tell me know all is right.

For if I try,
With all my might.
I can't hold off the enemy,
Till the dawn of light.

So I need you o' Lord,
I need You night and day.
In need to know You are there for me,
In a very special way.

To chase away my fears,
Just by a word You say.
Chase the enemy far from me,
In both night and day

Love Me Dear Lord

Love me dear Lord,
Love me today.
Love me with the love,
Only You can display.

I know the real and true love,
That You have for me.
Help me to display it,
So the whole world can see.

You promised that You would never leave us,
And I know that is true.
You said You would never forsake us,
And I believe that, too.

I need to grow closer to You,
This very day.
I need to be closer to You,
In every single way.

You love me so much,
That You died for me.
You love all You have created,
That is easy to see.

I know that You love even those,
That are lost.
I know love is the reason,
You died on the cross.

It was my sins you bore,
There on Calvary's hill.
It was Your blood that was spilled,
For our Father's will.

I must not forget to repent when I am wrong,
This I can't afford.
I must come to You daily for I know You love me,
My dear Lord.

At This Time For Rest

As I prepare for rest,
And lay down to sleep,
I ask You Lord for protection,
And my soul would You keep.

I need to know that in Your arms,
I will be through out the night.
Would you hold me Lord?
And do it with all Your might.

It's been a tough day Lord,
But You have been with me all the way.
Am I doing things right Lord,
Did I work for You today.

Sometimes I fear I missed some things,
You wanted me to do.
Will You give me sight Lord?
That I might see them through.

I want to dream of love,
And the wonderful things You have for me.
I know You want me to stay focused on You,
For that is surely the key.

I have one more thing Lord,
That I would ask of You.
All those that I love Lord,
Would you protect them, too?

For I know that Your love,
And protection is the very best.
Now I ask You to come to me,
At this time for rest.

Jesus, My Special Friend

My Dear Lord, You are so great,
And so very much divine.
You are the greatest friend,
I ever needed to find.

You blessed us with such love,
And Your wonderful spirit.
It's the gift of Your grace you give,
Without any merit.

You said for us to continue,
To be this very way.
So loving and humble,
From each day to day.

And if I forget this in my life,
At any time,
Please remind me that Your gifts,
Are purely divine.

I know You will stay with me,
And love me till my life's very end.
Please help to me grow closer to You,
From this day till then.

And I will live for You forever,
And with a smile upon my face.
And I will always be thankful for Your love,
And for Your saving grace.

For I love all your children,
The bad and the good.
I love them all,
Just as you said I would.

For all the sheep,
That have strayed far from Your flock,
Give me the strength to lead them back,
To Your solid rock.

To touch the wondering soul,
This gift to me You gave.
Give me strength to go,
And that my spirit will be brave.

For all the honor and glory,
I happily give back to You.
For it is not for me, but for You,
These things that I do.

Blessings For My Home

Good morning Lord,
I have a favor to ask of You.
It is straight forward Lord,
There is not anything You can't do.

Would You bless this place,
That I now call home?
You brought me here Lord,
No longer to roam.

I ask this from my heart Lord,
You know that is true.
I would not have a home Lord,
If it were not for You.

Would You bless this place Lord?
For You are so dear.
Would You bless all those too Lord,
Who would enter here?

Let all that enter here Lord,
Fill Your very presence and Your grace.
Fill their souls with Your spirit Lord,
When they come into this place.

Would You protect this place Lord,
That you have given to me?
I will give You the glory Lord,
And I shall honor thee.

This place that You have given to me,
Is more than just fine.
Would You fill this place with Your love Lord?
For it is so divine.

Would You cover my home Lord,
With a pure crystal dome?
I will praise You forever Lord,
For the blessings of my home.

I Shall Rejoice

You display Your love for me,
With the dawning of each and every day.
You draw me closer to You,
In every single way.

The blessings that You bestow on me,
Rock my very mind.
You show me daily that Your love,
Is truly one of a kind.

I praise You endlessly,
In my own special way.
You are the true and living God,
And with You I will always stay.

You bless me daily,
With all that You have for me.
Contentment is mine forever,
And I am as happy as can be.

You have given me peace,
And this I know comes from You.
Without Your love Lord,
I would not know what to do.

You did bring me to a fellowship,
That I love and they love You.
I can see Your precious Son,
In everything they do.

Thank You for my friends,
That have the love of Christ in their hearts.
They are my family Lord,
I am glad that we are not apart.

You bless me so much Lord,
Even when I do things I regret.
This is another day You have given me,
I shall rejoice and be glad in it.

God's Helpers

Thank you God for Jesus,
And for holding on to me,
For opening up my eyes,
And allowing me to see,

What wonderful love You have,
For all those of Yours.
Like Abraham and Job,
You open all the right doors.

As long as I wait,
And allow You to lead,
Things that are of this world,
I shall never need.

For heavenly things I know,
Is what You have for me.
Because worldly things are worthless,
This I can plainly see.

For those who can't speak to You,
As Father and as son,
Can't dream of all the things,
That You have perfectly done.

For when I am weak,
Christ will do for me Your loving will.
And I can feel and hear Him say,
My child, I love you still.

So when I get ill,
And want to do some sinful thing.
He speaks to me,
And I remember all the joy He can bring.

I love all those You use,
To speak Your words to me.
They make me so much stronger,
And I can remain totally free.

Chapter 2

Special Poems

My Darling Lori

My darling Lori you were so special,
The day you came into this world.
You were so beautiful,
And daddy had his precious little girl.

You had a tough time,
But I loved you with all my heart.
I knew right then,
That you and I would never ever part.

You had my skin, and eyes,
You were such a beautiful thing.
You are still a part of me,
And in my heart your name does ring.

Jesus said you must come live with him,
For now and for ever.
He said you would live for eternity;
Your life would end never.

I wish He would have taken me,
Instead of taking you.
But He knew what was best;
It was I who knew not what to do.

But I know that you are safe,
In His promised land.
And I will see you my darling Lori,
Just as soon as I can.

Thank you Lord for allowing her,
To visit me sometimes at night.
And when the morning comes, I smile,
For I know that she's alright.

She is my darling Lori Lord,
She is my shinning star.
I can't touch her now Lord,
But I know she is not that far.

And when my time on earth,
Has finally comes to an end.
I know you will have her waiting,
And together we will be again.

The Wall
(Dedication Poem)

As I was in D.C. today,
I came by to see your name.
It's been 40 years now,
And nothing is quite the same.

We were so young, you and I,
The day you went away.
How could we have known,
That it would all end this way?

As I was standing there,
Your bravery I started to recall.
You were a man's man;
You were always on the ball.

We all admired you very much,
For the responsibility that you bore.
Even as kids you stood up for us,
As it seemed to even the score.

After you fell I went there to that time,
And far away place.
It was like I was searching for you,
But I never saw your face.

We were fighters for freedom,
In a land where everyone was our foe.
But we have a taste for freedom now,
That the protected will never know.

So I'll say goodbye for now, I love you,
All of you have my respect.
I love to tell all the young soldiers now,
How freedom you did protect.

I just realized how much I miss you all,
My brave wonderful friends.
Your memories will live forever with me,
And never shall they end.

To the honor of all that fell with you,
In that far off place.
Their names will live on forever here,
And never shall be erased.

So if someone wants to know about real heroes,
I tell them about you all.
And if they want to meet you,
I tell them that you live in D.C. now, here at the wall.

The Preacher Man

I was preaching a sermon one Sunday,
Late last May.
The death clock was ticking,
Time was slipping away.

These folks were in trouble,
And one was about to die.
He said that he was innocent,
But they said that was a lie.

I was at a prison,
My congregation was in Jail.
One man seemed shaken,
And his face was very pale.

He was the very man,
They were about to put to death.
He looked like he had already taken,
His very last breath.

In the middle of the sermon this man came to me,
As I thought to pray.
He said "I am going to die tomorrow;
There is something I would like to say."

I asked him if he knew Jesus,
And if he was saved.
He said, "Oh yes preacher man,
I have victory over death, and the grave."

He said, "For many years I preached the gospel,
Just like you.
The warden said I could preach once more,
Before my life was through."

So I gave him the pulpit,
And quietly stepped to one side.
Some color came to his face,
And from his lips these words began to glide.

"I am going to die tomorrow,
They say for killing my wife.
But you guys know me,
You know I could never take a life."

You know they killed our blessed Jesus,
For something he didn't do.
I know how He must have felt,
For now they will kill to me, too.

Each one of you here has a desire,
To be free from this awful place.
You must come to this man and let him tell you,
About Jesus' saving grace.

Freedom is what He offers you,
And a new man you will become.
All this violence and hate will be taken from you,
By Gods only begotten Son.

After you die they will place you in the cold ground,
In this undesirable place.
Then Jesus will come and warm you with His love,
And with His grace.

When you profess Him as Lord you shall change,
And no more sin can you stand.
"Then you can rise and tell others to come,
And listen to this preacher man."

The Day Grandpa Went Away

It was on a Saturday,
The day Grandmother passed away.
I was just a little boy,
But it was clear what happened on that day.

I was on the floor playing,
When Daddy started to weep.
I asked, "what's wrong daddy?"
He said Grandma had gone to sleep.

That was in 1953,
And Grandpa was so big and strong.
I still hear him say to her,
"Going first, Ma, was oh so wrong."

You see he was working that day,
Out in the field.
Grandpa always worked hard,
The year he had a good yield.

It is now Christmas Eve 1963,
And we came to see Grandpa today.
We love to spend time with him,
He tells old stories some would say.

We came in the front door,
Of his old farm house.
Things were different that day;
It was quiet as a mouse.

Grandpa was in his rocker on the back porch,
And I heard him say,
"It's been ten long years Ma,
Since you went away.

The mule died last week,
And the tractor is broken down.
It looks like this entire farm,
Is about to fall to the ground.

I don't do as much around here,
Like I use to do.
I think my days of farming,
Are just about through.

I just don't want to do much anymore,
But sit and think of you.
It seems like only yesterday,
When we said I do.

I've not been feeling good Ma,
For a good many days.
I think my health is failing me,
In so many ways.

The kids are all ok and doing fine,
And the grandkids are, too.
Do you think they will get mad at me,
If I come to you?"

Grandpa went to sleep,
Later on that night.
He knew he would never see,
The coming of the morning light.

Now he's happy for Grandma he is with,
This Christmas day.
He'll tell her all the stories about what's gone on,
Since she's been away.

The Waterfall

As I sat by a waterfall,
Late one summer's day.
Thoughts of You pierced my soul,
In a very special way.

I thought how water flows freely,
After a fresh morning's rain.
And how love could flow just as easily,
And everyone would gain.
It was like I had known You,
For ever and a day.
It was clear You had been with me,
Every step of the way.

Can I maintain this feeling,
That You have allowed to begin.
And last till I get home to you,
And then start all over again?

You are so precious to me,
And I am so very glad we met.
And for answering Your call dear Lord,
I shall never, ever regret.

Far Over Daytona Beach

I arose early today,
So to get an early start.
Off to the golf course I go,
So I can load my brand new cart.

It is so pleasant this morning,
With a soft, warm breeze.
I hope we play well today,
And do it with ease.

Thank you Lord for giving me,
This another day.
Help me to see You in everything,
As we go to play.

Let me do something today,
That I have never done.
Maybe to get an eagle,
Or have a hole in one.

I love to rise early here,
To watch the birth of a new day.
Will You allow me to do this often,
If I see it in a special way?

To watch the day start is a blessing,
From You Lord I do beseech.
It is a grand thing to see the sun rise here,
Far over Daytona Beach.

The Warriors

As I sat at my desk gazing at my fathers portrait,
Hanging there on the wall.
The lives of the men in my family,
I started to recall.

My grandfather was in World War I,
And said that it was rough.
He said he saw a lot of people die
And that was really tough.

My father was a hero in World War II,
And he was wounded very bad.
His injuries took him at a young age,
And that was terribly sad.

My uncle went to Korea,
He was so brave and so bold.
He said the worst enemy that he had to fight,
Was the bitterness of the cold.

Then my turn came to go to war,
And a good soldier I would be.
I went to Vietnam,
And some horrible times I did see.

My grandfather left us,
In 1954.
The things that troubled his mind,
Would bother him no more.

My father would go 10 years later,
For he was in constant pain.
He was proud of his service,
And never once did he complain.

My uncle went too,
A year or two ago.
The frost bit he got there,
Really hurt him so.

I am still here,
And doing fairly fine.
My injuries were not as physical,
But they are still in my mind.

I want to be free of those things,
One day oh how I pray.
I want to be free from those battles,
On this very day

I am the last of the line of warriors,
That my family will send to die.
I and my brothers have no children,
This is the reason why.

One day I will join all those,
Who have gone on ahead of me.
Then I will be free from the things I had to do,
And the things I did see.

I pray there is a special place in Heaven,
For the patriots of this land.
To be in that place of peace and harmony,
Will make me a very happy, happy man.

A Dream Come True

As a new day starts tomorrow,
And I'm not there for you to wake.
You may ask yourself, where are you?
And tears you start to make.

Please sit and take a breath,
And allow a smile to take their place.
Think of the sweet love we shared,
And know that I finished the race.

I know the love you have for me,
For mine is the same for you.
I know you will often think of me,
And I know you will miss me. too.

If you only knew the peace I have,
You would truly understand.
That the Lord came and called my name,
And took me by the hand.

Don't dwell on the things,
We didn't take the time to say.
Just be happy for me,
That I am totally complete today.

Although I am in my mansion,
Here in Heaven far above,
Always remember when it comes to you,
So true was my love.

It was so hard to leave you,
For you made my life so bright.
I will always be there with you,
And caress you oh so tight.

I will be there in your mind,
And more so in your heart.
And know that beautiful smile you have,
Helps each day to start.

As I turned to leave you,
And start my journey home,
I thought of all the good we had,
And didn't think of the wrong.

And if I could return to yesterday,
Just for a little while,
I would tell you that I love you,
And see that beautiful smile.

As I approached almighty God,
Sitting there on His throne,
He smiled at me, I felt so blessed,
And knew I was really home.

Then I saw an amazing thing,
A great pile of golden crowns.
They were laid there before His son,
His precious Holy Lamb.

He gave me one and I held it there,
For just a little while.
Then I saw Him in His glory,
And place it on the pile.

He said that is for you,
For the good that you did achieve.
I said thank You Father, but this is His,
The one who delivered me.

Now I am really here with God,
And I am glad He called my name.
You keep smiling, and hold me close,
Until you hear the same.

Then we will be together again,
And forever here we shall stay.
Till then I promise to watch over you,
Until you reach that day.

Happiness

I watch people all the time,
As they move along their way.
They all look and will tell you,
They are happy most of the day.

Most will tell you that that life is good,
Smile and walk away.
But when they are at home all alone,
They know their not quiet that way.

Happiness is a feeling,
And it is here for you and me.
It survives in most folks,
Just look around and see.

When you wake in the morning,
Just stop and think right then.
Set your mind to the thought,
I will be happier than I have ever been.

Start off by talking to God,
And tell him your plan,
If He doesn't like it, He will let you know,
Then you can start all over again.

Happiness is easy to find,
Every day of the week.
You can find it today,
If it is happiness that you seek.

As you are talking with God,
Ask Him what it takes.
He will tell you to trust in Jesus,
For happiness is what He makes.

So be true to Him as you talk,
And As He looks into you heart.
And He will bless you as you ask,
Then you and happiness will never part.

He Lives

Lord as I sit here,
Writing this about you.
I ask that you help me,
And Lord would you bless it to.

As I recalled your word today,
I remember all the blessings that it gives.
As I speak of You I rejoice,
As I tell folks where my Savior lives.

Most say you live in heaven,
That is a place you will always be.
Some say you didn't exist,
And this really bothers me.

Some say that you don't live at all,
Some say you are in that cave,
Some think you died on old Calvary's hill.
And that cave was your finial grave.

These are the ones,
That never heard you say.
I knock would you let me in,
Here is where I want to stay.

He promised to never leave us,
This is His promise that He gives.
And if you would just look at my heart,
You would know that here is where He Lives.

God and Butterflies

As I come out to my spot in the garden,
To speak with God every morn.
I look for something new,
Something He allowed to be born.

It's early in the day,
The sun is about to rise.
As it appears above the horizon,
I see a new birth of butterflies.

It appears they dance to music,
That you and I can not hear.
They float around to angelic harps,
As they hold there cadence dear.

They float in and out ,
And they do it with such ease.
It is though they are riding so happily,
On God's gentle little breeze.

We should wake each morning,
And look for something new.
He will surprise most folks,
Just like he has me and you.

We could all do things in unison,
To beautify His creation.
We could do it peacefully and with love,
And not with rudeness or deviation.

Arise early in the morning to have a talk with Him,
He will show you things, without lies.
Or just set and watch the peace they share,
That's God and His butterflies.

Where Are You Lord

If you think that God has left you,
And to you He has gone away.
You had better stop and look inside,
For it is you who has gone astray.

He promised us He would never leave us,
Or in us depart.
He will never break the fellowship,
So you need to search your heart.

Many times we want to blame Him,
For our failing or things we lack.
He said our needs he'll always meet,
So you should get back on track.

If you should ask "Where are You Lord",
I'm sure you would hear Him say,
"I never left you my precious child,
It is you who went away."

So call on Him if you miss Him,
And hear His wonderful voice.
"Thank you for calling on me," He'll say,
"You made the wisest choice."

The Places I Would Love To Bring You

I would love to bring you places,
That you have never been.
Places that you could cherish,
From even now to then.

I would love to bring you to England,
Where the landscape is so bold.
To see the things of that country,
That are pristine and old.

To go to New England for the summer,
Would be so very neat.
To be there during the foliage season,
Would be so peaceful and sweet.

To be in Mexico down by the sea,
On a warm winter's day,
Where the sky is blue, the food is good,
And the water is really okay.

To see the mountains of Alaska,
Would be a wonderful time.
This is one of the greatest places,
That I love to call all mine.

To see the mountains capped with snow,
And the valleys richly green.
It is one of the most beautiful places,
That I have ever seen.

There's no place that can be as nice,
As the place I have waiting for you.
There are mansions bright, and streets of gold,
And lots of things to do.

It's a place called Heaven,
And there you can see Me and know that I am true.
For this is the very best place I have,
That I would love to bring you to.

That Special Sunday

Everyone was going to church;
It was a beautiful Sunday morn.
Except for one little girl,
Whose only dress was all tattered and torn.

She sat outside the church,
Behind a bush where no one could see.
She watched as everyone entered,
And said, "Oh I wish that could be me."

As she stood and was ready to leave,
A man walked up by her side.
He said, "Don't weep my child, you're not alone,
It was for you that I died."

She smiled at Him and went inside,
And there she knelt to pray.
All the others were so amazed,
When they heard the little girl say,

"Thank you Lord for all you have done,
And for loving me this way.
Thank you Lord for all You have done,
And for coming to me today."

So when you are down and out,
You can count on He who died.
To come to you and comfort you,
And stand by your side.

So when you go into a church,
Stop and think to pray.
And He will come and comfort you,
And there He will always stay.

Precious In The Eyes Of The Lord
(Psalm 116:15)

When someone gets a disease,
Folks get down and really sad.
We say oh how pitiful this is,
This is very, very bad.

We call them victims,
Oh what a dreadful word.
Why not call them saints?
For this have they never heard.

We say they are terminal;
There is nothing we can do.
We will try to keep them comfortable,
Till their very life is through.

We are asked to pray that You will heal them,
And take away the pain.
We should know You do this,
For this is your very aim.

You heal them that belong to You,
In every single way.
You call them into Your presence,
Every hour of every day.

Painless and free of trials,
Are all those who go to Him.
They are in a heavenly bliss;
This is the promise He has made to them.

When the Dr's say I am finished,
And a miracle healing is what I need.
Be assured that the process has started,
Just sit with me and read.

They say that the hearing,
Is the very last thing to go.
So from His word please read,
For I will be listening to you, you know.

Tell them I don't know where victims go,
I guess they are just gone.
But you can tell them this saint is healed,
And on his journey home.

Not For Sale

We all must remember,
That things don't always work out.
Just stay focused on Jesus,
For He is what it is all about.

In the shadows Satan does lurks,
He hides and waits to attack.
So don't let down your guard,
And let him get you back.

Satan can make you feel,
That worldly things are oh so grand.
And everything you want,
Can be right in the palm of your hand.

A brand new car, a brand new home,
Oh it looks so good.
But what a price you'll pay,
For some chrome and pieces of wood.

How about life itself,
That too he can do for you.
Break a heart, bust up loves,
What more would he have you do?

The list goes on, and I am sure,
Of all the things he'll promise you.
So you better think of the price you'll pay,
When payment time comes due.

Satan's price is high, but Jesus doesn't charge,
And He will never fail.
So start today and choose our Lord,
And tell Satan you're not for sale.

Father's Day

It has been 46 years,
Since Dad went away.
I still miss him so,
Especially on Father's Day.

This year was to be the worse,
For I was all alone.
Our family is not here anymore,
Away they all have gone.

As Father's day approached this year,
I was full of fears.
For I did not want to be alone,
And my eyes filled with tears.

Then my friend called,
And said she was coming to spend the day with me.
All day long we were together,
And so happy I would be.

She said that she wanted to be with me,
And we had lots to do.
We had lunch, and dinner,
And watched a baseball game, too.

This was the best Father's Day,
I have had since Jesus called him home.
She made me so glad to be alive,

I still wish he could be here,
To spend each and ever day.
I love him so and I know,
That with me he will forever stay.

Now I have a special person,
That fills my heart with happiness.
I know he would love her, too,
For she brings love, smiles and kindness.

Dad, she was sent to me,
By Almighty God or maybe even you,
To brighten my life again,
And she said she loves me, too.

She has filled my heart with love again,
And I am glad to have her here.
Who ever in heaven sent her,
Would you thank them my father dear?

I now look forward to Father's Day,
To come around next year.
She will make it special for me,
And I have nothing more to fear.

When our time on earth is done,
And our work here is through,
It will be so great Dad,
To introduce this special lady to you.

What A Blessing You Are

Not many has God blessed,
Like He has blessed you.
You are a blessing,
In everything you do.

He gave you a wonderful spirit,
That was His special way.
You must show it to the world,
Every single day.

You are a blessing,
To everyone you meet.
Even to a stranger,
That you pass on the street.

When people look at you,
It is like seeing the rising sun.
In you people can see,
The results of the risen One.

You are a blessing to your family,
And very much to me.
Your blessings could easily fill,
God's grandest sea.

God has blessed you in so many ways,
It isn't hard to say.
I pray God will bless me,
That I may hear from you today.

Honest To The Core

We like to think that we are wise,
By all the things we do.
We make decisions that are not very good,
Or very well thought through.

We don't think about others,
Or how they will react.
If they question us on what we want,
We go on the attack.

We must understand that folks are different,
In the ways they think.
We must look through their eyes,
And then take time to blink.

We don't want to hurt others,
By the things we say or do.
Some get very angry if they hear,
"I don't agree with you."

Slow down and think about what they need,
And don't fuel their rage.
Try harder to understand what they feel,
And get to the very same page.

Making fast decisions can be hurtful,
And drive you far apart.
We must always think of the ones we love,
And speak from our heart.

If we remain calm with each other,
And try to understand,
Everyone will gain from it,
Every woman and every man.

To have a loving heart is worthless,
If it is not correctly used.
A loving heart is tremendous,
If it does not abuse.

Think what a tangled web,
We do surely weave,
When our minds over rule our hearts,
And we attempt to deceive.

When we don't care if we don't agree,
And we think they are a bore,
We must remember to be open and true,
And even honest to the core.

Music From The Air

As I was idle today,
I saw birds that flew with amazing grace.
What sweet songs they sing,
As they build their nesting place.

When their songs are in my heart,
So swiftly pass the days.
The troubles of life depart,
And leave lots of time for praise.

They work with dedication,
And I pray coldness will not come,
Until the music makers of the air,
Get their homes completely done.

My job today seems like play,
And all day long I can rejoice.
If I need cheering up,
I can listen to the sweetness of their voice.

Just as the birds are so happy,
As they work and as they sing,
I hear their heavenly songs,
And happiness to me they bring.

As I see them work,
And hear the tenderness of their songs,
They seem to do it all just right,
And avoid all the wrongs.

Will you allow me to watch the birds,
And all that they do,
Will you allow the birds to sing for me,
And allow others to hear them too?

For they bring happiness to my soul,
When their music I strive to hear.
And as they sing their songs for me,
The glory of you My Lord is so very, very clear.

My Patio

I love sitting on the patio,
At this place of mine.
This is where I greet my neighbors,
In the morning time.

Many ask the question,
Just what it is I do.
I tell them that I write poetry,
And it all comes from you.

Some say that is great,
And some just look kind of weird.
Some want to see my work,
Some act a little scared.

Some stop and chat for a while,
Some just walk on by.
Some will smile and say hello,
Some will nod and give a little sigh.

Some just don't understand,
And think that I am crazy.
Some think that I do nothing,
And am a little lazy.

Most are nice and speak kindly,
When they walk by.
Some are troubled,
And appear like they are about to cry.

I can tell who knows You,
And Your blessed Son.
Some read my poems and say "yes,
This is what He done."

I want to tell them all just who Jesus is,
With a tremendous shout.
For they all need to know who He is,
And what He is all about.

So I will continue in the morning,
To sit on my patio.
So to all that pass by I can smile,
Wave and say hello.

And to all of those that ask me,
Just what is it I do,
I will gladly smile and tell them,
That I gratefully work for You.

What Will You Do

A day will come when the lord will say;
Your work here is through.
When you find yourself in his presence,
Will you know what to do?

We like to think that we know,
What will go on that finial day.
Do we really know what we will do
Or what, we will say.

Think of it and you will find how hard it is,
Just to think it through.
For we do not fear the lord,
In the ways that we really ought to.

Just ask yourself what you would do,
If you heard God say.
I am going to bring you home my child,
And I am going to do it today.

Would you say oh God, I am not ready;
There are things here not though.
I have thought of this for a long, long time,
And this is what I hope to do.

I hope to be in a hurry,
And in a very big way.
For so long I have been waiting,
For this very day.

I will run by Paul, Peter,
And Bartholomew.
I will run by Mark, Luke,
And Matthew too.

I will want to talk to them all,
For I will be there at last.
And as I run by them, I will smile,
And wave so very fast.

I will shout I don't want to be rude,
Or show bad behavior.
I just need to see the Lamb of God,
The one who is my savior.

Beyond Tampa Bay

As I sit this evening,
In awe of the setting sun.
I see a portrait that was painted,
By the risen one.

He shows us daily of all the things,
He alone has done.
This artist is the Holy one,
God's only begotten son.

It is so clear to me,
His authority is everywhere.
It is over here you see,
And, look, it is also over there.

You can see it in the flowers, birds,
And in the swaying trees.
You can see it in His people,
And in the honey bee's.

He is so gracious, as daily He shows us,
The trueness of His love.
It is as clear and straight,
As the flight of His turtle dove.

He has made all these things,
For the goodness of His will.
And even when we do wrong,
We know He loves us still.

It is hard for most to recognize,
His touch on all that we view.
If we stop and think, all will know,
That it had to come from You.

Just look around you tomorrow,
And see Him in this way.
Or just sit and watch the sun as it sets,
Far beyond Tampa Bay.

Love Flows Like A River

Love is like a river,
That flows every single day.
It brings freshness to its shores,
While it travels along its way.

Its water is cool when it flows true,
It's calm and never gets too bold.
This is the way it should be,
For this is well with my soul.

Love brings newness to all those around you,
And this will never change.
This love comes from God,
And brings joy to all within your range.

When my love ones come to me,
And love is what they need.
They can see my love for them,
For this is my willing deed.

Always show to those you love,
Just how much you they mean to you.
Curtsey and humbleness,
Will mean the world to them too.

Like the river that flows to us,
From God every single day.
Should be shown to those around you,
And they will love you in a very special way.

The Gathering

It wasn't so long ago,
We all lived close by.
We would play with each other,
Laugh, tease, and also cry.

As children we learned,
The strong values of our friends.
We would link them close to our soul,
With loyalty that never ends.

When we would grow older,
And our own lives we would lead.
We would never forgot our childhood friends,
Especially when there was a need.

Our own talents that God gave to us,
We would put to work for their sake,
To paint a house, or start a car,
Whatever it would take

Let's have a dinner,
Someone would say.
Let's invite all our friends,
And have a marvelous day.

We will all be happy as can be,
With the stories we are sharing
We shall all honor and call this day,
A Day of The Gathering.

The Day We All Come Back Together

It was 40 years ago when this group,
Was last all together.
They said that they would stay in touch.
Lose that connection never.

But somehow the mighty winds,
Began to steadily blow.
Where we all would end up,
Not many of us would know.

Some would stay in our home town,
But many could not stay.
Most would be off to college.
Or off to be in harms way

Most all would marry,
And find a career
Some would stay at home,
And raise there family dear.

But throughout all the years,
They all remembered there friends,
They would all join in.
When ones troubles seem not to end.

They would pray, call, and be in support,
And ask what else I can do.
The replay would be easy,
You have done enough I surely love you.

When a person thinks,
They are all alone and it is the end
They need to stop and look around,
And see all their friends.

They will come and support you
Now matter the hardships, or the harshness of weather
And I will never forget this time and place
The day we all come back together

The Love of A Woman

Today I was thinking,
Of the women in my life.
My Grammy, Mother,
And especially my wife.

I thought how some men say,
Without them we can do.
I don't think we can,
After all they naturally do.

The love of a woman,
Is a wonderful thing to see.
She is God's gift to man,
And she is all He intended her to be.

She's the one who holds us together,
With her knowledge and her love.
She is the one who teaches us,
As gracefully as the flight of a dove.

She is the one the world depends on,
To be kind and oh so steady.
She is the care giver to her family,
The one who is always ready.

Some say that mothers favor the boy,
And others say the girl.
I know that the hands that rocks the cradle,
Also rules the world.

God placed such love within a woman,
That a man can not clutch.
You can see it in her eyes, her smile,
And you can feel it in her touch.

She has a deeper love,
Than anything on the earth.
There isn't anything she wouldn't do,
To protect those which she has given birth.

At the same time she will teach, discipline,
And show them the ways of her own.
She will follow them and groom them,
Till well after they are grown.

To her man she will stick too,
Till the very end.
Her love for him is solid,
It will never wavier or ever bend.

For this woman that God made for us,
We should love and cherish them all that we can.
If you want to see some of God's finest work,
Just watch the love of a woman.

My Home Town

It has been a long, long time,
Since I left my home town.
To look for that pot of gold,
That never have I found.

It seems like 40 years,
That I have been away.
As I look back it has been,
40 years almost to the day.

I left to serve my country,
Right after high school.
To serve our country,
Was daddy's golden rule.

After the war,
I didn't stay here very long.
I roamed around the world,
Could I have been so wrong.

My career was great,
I loved my work so well.
But it seems my friends missed me,
But this I couldn't tell.

When the time come,
That I was sick and very much alone.
My friends called and said,
Why don't you come home.

They said they loved me,
And they wanted me around.
So today I am on a road trip,
Back to my home town.

Chapter 3

Devotional Poems

The Creator

Genesis

(Day 1)

You made the whole world with just a word,
And a thought.
You made it all,
And none of it was bought.

You made it great,
Without a worry or a sigh.
You made the earth round,
And blue you made the sky.

You then made a light,
And you made it to shine so bright.
It would shine in the day,
And it would also shine at night.

You just thought about it,
As You knew that You would.
And when You saw it all,
You said this is very good.

You made it all,
In Your very own way.
And when You had finished,
It was the end of the very first day.

(Day 2)

You commanded a gap between the waters,
So Your creation may be clear.
This will be a great thing for all,
And we shall hold it oh so dear.

For the things that You shall create next,
Shall hold a special place.
For each will have a special reason,
And all of it shall show Your face.

There shall be the sky,
Where all things of the universe shall be.
And they will be oh so lovely,
For every eye to see.

"This is what I will do,"
Is what God did say.
"And when I finish this,"
It shall be the end of the second day.

(Day 3)

"I shall make a world,
And it shall be so fine.
I will separate the sea and land,
And all will see Me as loving and kind.

Parts will be dry; this shall be the land,
Where My creations shall live.
There will be plants and seeds for planting,
They will abundantly give.

They shall be used as nourishment,
And healthy they will stay.
They will live in a paradise,
This is what I say.

I will make strong My creations,
So they will love Me all the way.
And when I do this it will be the end,
Of only the third day."

(Day 4)

"I will make lights in heaven far above,
And they shall shine so bright.
One will rule the day,
And the other will rule the night."

He said they would be our daily guides,
For all of us to walk by.
And He would set them in the right place,
Both high in the sky.

God knew that these lights,
Would help you and me.
They will keep us warm,
And there light will help us see.

They are still there,
Just like He did say.
And when it was done,
It was the end of the fourth day.

(Day 5)

God said "Let there be animals on the land,
And living things in the sea.
God said "Let them become many,
And to fill the world as quick as can be."

So all the living things were there,
To live in this place.
And all did grow and fill the earth,
And a smile was on God's face.

Now there were living things,
On this place that God did make.
This place was His,
And this was no mistake.

All that God wanted,
Was here to stay.
And when they were complete,
It was the end of the fifth day.

(Day 6)

God made it all,
And it was so very, very good.
He made it all just the way,
He knew that He should.

He made all the living things,
And they covered the earth.
He made each a mate of its own kind,
So they could generate birth.

Then He made a man,
That was to be like Him.
And He created woman,
He created both of them.

To govern over everything else,
That He made and He did say.
"I will make it easy for you,
And this I will do today."

God said, "All this I will give to you,
So you will have food to live.
I will make you plants for grain,
This I gladly give."

All this was done,
And it was good He did say.
He smiled at His creations,
And it was the end of the sixth day.

(Day 7)

Now God had finished His creation,
And all was in its place.
He looked it all over,
And peace came to His face.

He had done all this with just a thought,
And a word to say.
So God blessed His creation,
And rested, for this was the seventh day.

GO
(Matt 28:19-20)

Devotional

He came to us,
Late in the day.
He said, "I have something important,
Listen to what I say.

My father has given me authority,
Over all that I do.
He has trusted me with this,
And I now I will trust it with you."

He said, "go into all the lands,
And tell them of Me.
Tell them to learn quickly,
And I will set them free."

"Tell them The Great I Am,
His Son and His Spirit.
Have a gift for them and it's free of cost,
Or without any merit.

Have them to learn all,
That you have seen Me do.
Then tell them to teach others,
So more can be saved, too.

Do not worry about the places,
You must go on this earth.
I will be with you, and protect you,

A Place Called Calvary
(Mark 15:37)

Devotional

There is a place called Calvary,
Where people were killed, most were bad.
That's where the promised Messiah died,
And that was oh so sad.

They made a cross of wood,
And there He died nailed on a Dogwood tree.
This man was a sacrifice you see,
For He died for you and me.

For our sins He laid down His life,
So that we can be saved.
He won the victory that day,
Over death and the grave.

He said no greater thing can one do,
Than to die for a friend.
This He did for us,
So our lives would never ever end.

He wants us to love others,
With the love He has for us.
And that is to help and care for them,
And never fight or fuss.

For His love is pure,
And totally divine.
This kind of love can be yours,
For it is already that of mine.

So think it over,
And you will surely find,
That love like His,
Is one that is oh so kind.

So prepare your heart and soul,
With love like He has for you and me.
For you may never know when your day may come,
To go to your Calvary.

The Changed Man
(Mark 9:2-10)

Devotional

Some time had passed,
And Jesus took three away for a little walk.
There were just the four them,
And to them Jesus needed to talk.

Something grand was about to happen to Him,
By the Father from on high .
Witnesses he needed for He wanted them to see
His deity was no lie.

Peter, James, and John saw Jesus changed,
And they saw how it was done.
His garments became white as snow,
And His face shone like the sun.

And then two from the past were there greeting,
And talking with him.
It was Moses and Elias,
And the disciples recognized both of them.

The three didn't know what to do,
So Peter started to speak.
His thinking wasn't just right,
And his voice was probably weak.

Then a cloud appeared,
And their complete attention it did seize.
When a voice said, "This is my beloved son,
With whom I am well pleased."

The three were so scared they fell to the ground,
And appeared as dead.
Then Jesus came to them,
And rubbed them on their trembling heads.

Arise and do not be afraid,
For no harm will come to you.
They all have gone away for now,
And I will tell you what you must do.

As they were on their way back,
And He explained something to the three.
Soon I will be joining the ones you saw,
For that is My destiny.

When we get back, tell no one what you saw,
Or what was said,
Until the day comes,
That I rise from the dead.

The Harvest
(Matt 9: 35-38)

Devotional

Jesus did not stay in one place long,
He was always on the move.
He had places to go, people to heal,
His deity he wanted to prove.

He was telling them of a place,
That was real and it was at hand.
It was a place of righteousness,
Just as his Father had planned.

Making folks whole, and healing the sick,
What a wonderful thing.
They would follow Him, tell others,
His praises they would sing

They appeared to be lost,
And knew not their own way.
But He knew what to do,
And He knew just what to say.

Then He said to the twelve,
"Your work is here for you.
There's a lot of sheep to gather,
And you know what to do.

They need to be gathered,
So in my Fathers pasture they will stay.
There are many that are lost,
That you can see here today.

Ask with a pure heart,
For our Father will hear your call.
He will tell you just what we need,
And this will be good for all.

Ask and He will lead those to spread the gospel,
All through the land.
Have them to tell all to repent,
For the kingdom of God is at hand."

The Model From The Model
(Matt 6:9-13)

Devotional

When I speak to you Father,
I do it as a respectful son.
This is what You deserve,
After all You have done.

Your throne room is in its place,
And You are in control over me.
Your name is more honorable,
Than anything I know or can see.

This is Your spiritual reign,
Ours is in the reign of Jesus Your Son.
I will not resign myself to fate,
But your perfect purpose be done.

I know You will supply my every need,
This word You did say.
You give more so I can give to others;
This is Your precious way.

Forgive me Father if I do something,
That's not just right.
I will forgive others if I see wrong,
In my narrow sight.

Deliverance from Satan and his deceit,
Is what I pray.
Chase this evil from my path Lord,
Thru these words I say.

For the kingdom is Yours Father,
And Yours alone.
You have promised it to Your heirs I know,
But Yours alone is the throne.

All the glory in the world,
Does belong to You.
It is Yours forever father,
This is what I believe is true.

God's Lamb
(various)

Devotional

As God looked down,
On man one time.
He said this is the best creation,
Of all of Mine.

They worked in the quarries,
And made things of tin.
But man was mean to each other,
And begin to live in sin.

Man would come to the temple,
As to worship the Lord.
But man broke God's heart,
Many seemed calloused and bored.

God saw man was weak,
And for help he would not call.
So He sent his only Son,
to be the Savior for all.

That sacrificial lamb,
Which God did send,
A victory over death and the grave,
He did win.

Even though He died for us,
He arose to life again.
So a choice we could have,
For a new life to begin.

The reason for Him to die,
Seemed to be wrong and no good.
But they meant to kill Him anyway,
As He knew they would.

So He went back to his Father,
But we shall see Him again.
For He shall return to claim His own,
From this world of sin.

He will take us from here,
To our mansions on streets of gold.
A place He has prepared for us,
Just as He has told

He hears us when we cry out,
When we are troubled and low.
And He will come to us with all haste,
For His tender love to show.

So when that time comes on you,
And you feel lonely and blue.
Just call on God's Lamb,
And He will come and comfort you.

Never Doubt
(Matt 14:22-33)

Devotional

"Into the vessel now," Jesus did say,
"Privacy soon is what I need."
So they entered the ship as He wished, committed,
And with very great speed.

"To yonder shore,
You must sail.
While I tend to these here,
For them I must not fail."

"Go your way now," He said to the crowd,
"I have something I must do.
There will be tomorrow,
This I promise you."

They all being filled,
Did go there own way.
But they knew Jesus would be there tomorrow,
A promise He did say.

Jesus always found time,
To be with His Father all along the way.
He had to talk with Him,
Every single day.

Jesus was by Himself,
When the end of the day did come.
All afternoon He was with his Father,
This is what He done.

The sea was rough,
And the little vessel was in the middle.
The waves were very large,
And the boat was oh so little.

Jesus went to them,
For it was now late at night.
He wanted to make sure,
That the 12 were alright.

Bothered they were,
When they saw something on the sea.
They marveled and wondered,
Just what that could be.

Being afraid they started to cry,
It's a ghost we think.
He has come to take us,
We shall surely sink.

But the love of the Lord calmed them,
When He said, "be of good cheer.
It is me be happy,
There is no danger here."

Then ole Peter not believing his eyes,
Said, "Lord is it really you.
Allow me to walk on the water,
Allow me come to You."

The Lord said, "Come to me Peter,
And see that it is I."
Peter stepped out of the boat,
And walked, then the wind did blow high.

As he started to sink,
"Save me Lord" Peter did shout.
Jesus must have shaken his head,
And said, "what is this all about."

Jesus grabbed Peter by the hand,
And pulled him from the sea.
Jesus said, "O thou of little faith,
Why do you not trust in Me?

All the teaching,
I did freely give unto you.
Embrace them with all your might,
And focus upon Me in all that you do."

The Promises
(Matt 5:3-11)

Devotional

Just look at the blessed Son,
Who instructs us on just what to do.
Riches here are worthless,
Lasting wealth is what is waiting for you.

Let your heart be at peace,
When you are weak and even cry.
For the love of our Lord will come to you,
He is always very close by.

When all the old things,
Have passed away,
The Lord will make all things new,
And there we will stay.

If you seek Him first,
You shall never hunger or thirst.
Seek His kingdom too;
For He said seek this first.

Love all He made,
And you will be feel His tender touch.
For His mercy is great,
For He loves you oh so much.

Train the mind He has given you,
And you will see His face.
You will be in His presence,
In that wonderful place.

Pure has no imperfections,
It is solid as gold.
I believe every word,
That my God has already told.

If you are a disciple of Christ,
You will teach and live by love.
A child of His you will be,
And He will bless you with all from above.

Be assured that peace is not far away,
And will cover you like a dome.
For His kingdom will be yours,
The second He calls you home.

Study to show yourself approved,
And concentrate on the very best.
For Almighty God said if you do this,
You will be eternally blessed.

Happy Will Be My Days

"Happy Monday"

It may be hard to be happy,
On the first day of the work week.
But you can do it easily,
If it is happiness that you seek.

The weekend is over,
And Sunday is gone.
Be happy for today,
That you are not all alone.

"Happy Tuesday"

I feel much better,
About today.
I can now think how good it was,
Yesterday.

I had no bad feelings,
Or thoughts of sorrow.
I can hardly wait,
Until tomorrow.

"Happy Wednesday"

Today is hump day,
And it is all down hill from here.
I have been so happy this week,
My heart is full of cheer.

I am so glad I decided to be happy,
Every single day.
Only the love of God,
Can make me this way.

"Happy Thursday"

Today,
I will help someone in need.
To give a friendly smile,
Or look for someone to feed.

I want to tell everyone,
That being happy is no sin.
Just turn it over to Jesus,
And let it all begin.

"Happy Friday"

Friday is here at last,
And toil for the week is done.
I think I will call some friends,
And have a bit of fun.

I will tell them how happy,
I have been every day this week.
And tell them that,
Jesus is the One they should seek.

"Happy Saturday"

It is the first day off,
And I feel so grand.
I am so happy about life,
I can hardly stand.

This has been one of the best weeks,
Of my entire life.
Christ took my burdens, unhappiness,
And all of my strife.

"Happy Sunday"

It is early,
On Sunday morn.
Much like the day,
That Jesus was born.

I will seek His presence.
And special thanks I'll give Him today.
For it is His special love,
That has made me feel this way.

The 5 K
(Matthew 14:1- 21)

Devotional

When Herod was king,
It was a tough time for all under his reign.
They had everything to loose,
And very little to gain.

He had it all, lots of the finest food to eat,
And the best wine to drink.
He was arrogant, too;
It didn't matter to him what anyone else would think.

He had John the Baptist in jail for preaching,
And death was on its way.
Herrodis had his head cut off,
Because she hated what he had to say.

After this was done, John's friends came,
And took him away.
They would bury the Baptist then find Jesus,
To see what He would say.

When the disciples found Jesus,
They didn't feel very hearty.
Then they told Him how John was killed,
At Herod's birthday party.

When Jesus heard, He withdrew,
And wanted to be alone.
He was probably very sad now,
That His cousin was dead and gone.

Then Jesus entered a boat,
And then they sailed away.
The crowds heard what happened,
And followed Him along the way.

When Jesus landed, He saw lots of people,
And some were very ill.
Out of His compassion,
He healed them for that was His loving will.

It is now late in the day,
And they were not near a town.
He was told to send them away,
So food could be found.

Jesus said, "No sit them down,
And get them off their feet.
Share your food with them,
So now we all can eat."

They told Jesus, "we only have 5 pieces of bread,
And two little fishes."
Jesus said, "Bring them to Me,
That will be a great deal of dishes."

Jesus took the food and blessed it,
To the glory of the Fathers will.
And all five thousand men did eat,
Until they had their fill.

Now women and children,
Were not counted in that day.
But Jesus fed them, too;
He was going to have His way.

You don't have to be a king,
To feast like one you see.
Just count on Jesus for He has enough,
To feed even you and me.

Why Do We Worship The Lord
(various)

Devotional

Jesus said that we should worship God,
And only Him shall we serve.
He is the creator of all things,
Worship is what he deserves.

He made the whole world,
With just a single thought.
He made everything perfect,
Nothing here was bought.

He made man,
On the sixth day.
He made him whole,
What else can I say?

He made him in His image,
Even till this very day.
He made man like Himself
That was His way.

He made light so the darkness,
Could not be in control.
He made the seasons,
So in the Son we could stroll.

He made the rain,
So our crops could drink and grow.
He made scriptures,
So how to live we would know.

He made Lucifer,
But he fell into sin.
He made Jesus,
So the victory He could win.

He made me and you to live for Him,
Or die by the sword.
Freely He gives eternal life;
This is why we worship the Lord.

To Honor The Lord
(Psalm 23)

Devotional

He is my caregiver;
There is nothing that I need.
He gives me rest in a pasture,
Sowed from His fresh, new seed.

He gives me drink new,
Fresh and cold.
He gives me a new life,
When this one has grown tired and old.

Because of Your name,
I must walk upright.
When it appears that death is around me,
You are always in my sight.

You are my strength,
To fight off wrong.
They are my weapons,
All the day long.

You give me everything,
To overthrow the evil one.
I am covered by Your blood,
You saw that this was done.

You have blessed me,
With all I have gained in time.
But when my time comes,
All the victories will be surely Thine.

That house not built with hands,
Will be mine forever.
And I shall always be there,
To leave it never.

What Is The Word
(various)

Devotional

The word is the inspired voice of God;
We should learn it.
The word is the unlimited truth;
We should teach it.

The word is the music of our hearts;
We should sing it.
The word is to be shared with the world;
We should preach it.

The word is essential; that's why,
We should learn it.
The word is trustworthy; that's why,
We should teach it.

The word is the song of our souls; that's why,
We should sing it.
The word is priceless to our lives; that's why,
We should preach it.

The word is the walk that we should walk; that's why,
We should learn it.
The word is the language we should speak; that's why,
We should teach it.

The word is praise that we should give Him; that's why,
We should sing it.
The word is the life we should lead; that's why,
We should preach it.

The Forgiver
(Various)

Devotional

Once there was a man paralyzed,
And lying on a bed.
He was so bad he almost appeared,
To be fully dead.

His friends took him up on the roof,
So Jesus could see.
And Jesus said,
"Your faith is much,"
Your sins are forgiven thee.

There was a woman,
Who was unfaithful to her man?
The leaders wanted to kill her,
But Jesus knelt and wrote in the sand.

Jesus ask, "Who of you are without sin?"
And it hit them to the core.
And Jesus said to the woman,
"I condemn thee not, go and sin no more."

A lady washed Jesus' feet in oil,
And dried them with her hair.
And those who were eating with the Lord,
Didn't want the lady there.

The lady had fear,
Because she thought they would make her cease.
Jesus said to her, "Thy faith has saved thee,
Now "go in peace"

A girl asked Peter,
"Are you a disciple of this man here?"
"I am not" Peter said,
"And this I want to make perfectly clear."

It was cool that night, so he stood by the fire,
As to warm his hand.
Others around the fire were talking about this Jesus,
A miracle man.

They asked Peter, "are you a disciple of this man,
Who's causing this fuss?"
"I am not" Peter did say,
"He does not know any of us."

A man that Peter had cut off his ear,
Said, "You were with him."
Peter said, "Once again you are wrong,
I was not with them."

Jesus then asked Peter, "Do you love me?"
Three times Peter said, "Yes Lord I do."
Jesus said, "Then follow Me,
For Peter I love you, too."

There were three on the cross,
On Calvary's famous hill.
They were there to die,
Them they had to kill.

One said naught the other said, "Remember me,
When your time does come."
Jesus said, "For this day,
You will be with Me in my Father's kingdom."

Then the time came when Jesus would die,
Just as they knew.
Jesus said,
"Forgive them,, to his Father, "For they know not what they do."

So when you are wrong,
And your conscience won't let you out the door.
Call on the Forgiver,
He will come and say go and sin no more.

He Speaks
(Matt 7:21-24a)

Devotional

Why do we call on Him,
And do things in His name?
Not all those who do shall live with Him,
For they are not the same.

But if we strive,
To do our Father's will,
In His kingdom we shall live,
And this is bound with a seal.

No matter how many call on Jesus,
In that day and time,
And tell all they've done for him,
With all reason and rhyme.

They will say we did this,
Or we did that.
But it will make no difference,
What they try to pull from their hat.

They may have worked hard,
But for themselves they toiled.
Not for the sake of Christ,
Their party will be spoiled.

They may have worked,
Yes or maybe no.
But He will tell them, "I know you not,
Now you must go."

"Go from me now,"
He will say.
"Work for your own master,
And join him today."

"If you have an ear, listen,
To what I say and do obey.
For I am the truth, the life,
And the only way."

Paul Said
(Various)

Devotional

Paul said to pray without ceasing.
This will ever to God's love, be increasing.

Paul said the love of money is the root of all evil.
If you place your faith in this, you are surely from the devil.

Paul said let no one deceive themselves for naught.
Wisdom of the world is death, wisdom in Christ is what we are taught.

Paul said do not quench the spirit of Jesus.
The spirit of God, is the comforter for all of us.

Paul said to rejoice in your suffering.
We will learn and become stronger, with out any buffering.

Paul said we walk by faith not by sight.
We walk by His faith, by day and by night.

Paul said to preach the word in season and out of season.
Preach the word of God, each time you can for any reason.

Paul said for we brought nothing into this world and we shall take nothing
out.
Why do we fight for earthly things, when it carries no clout?

When you are in trouble, or have some sort of terrible thought,
Read what Paul said, and see what for you, Jesus has bought.

Seven Last Comments
(various)

Devotional

Father, forgive them; for they know not what they do.
They have no idea why this they have to do.
Would You bless them Father and would You forgive them, too?

Verily I say unto Thee, today shalt Thou be with me in paradise.
Two more were there with the blessed Son on that redemption day.
One of them was given a promise to be with Him when he went away.

Woman, behold thy Son!
He told Mary to look at her Son,
She could hardly look for all they had done.

Behold thy mother!
Then he told John to look at his mother.
John embraced her like he had no other.

I thirst.
Then He that was nailed to the tree there on Calvary's hill,
Asked for a drink of water, but with vinegar the sponge they did fill.

It is finished.
He looked into the eyes of all who could see,
And he said, "It is over, you have the whole of Me."

Father, into thy hands I commend my spirit.
Then He spoke to His Father, His voice was like thunder and did roll,
He said, "To Your hands of mercy I commit My very soul.

He Arrives
(Matthew 3)

Devotional

"Repent for the kingdom of heaven is at hand,"
John the Baptist did say.
"Believe in Him that comes after me,"
For He is the only way.

He is the Christ the son of God,
And He must surly grow. .
Follow Him for I am but a mere man,
This you surly know.

He is the holy One,
Whose shoes I am not worthy to unlace.
This one is the Son of God,
You will feel His love, and His saving grace.

He is the promised Messiah,
And He has come here to save.
Listen to Him dear Israel,
For He will defeat death and the grave.

I baptize you with water unto repentance,
For this is His desire.
But He that comes will baptize thee,
With the Holy Ghost and fire.

Then He came to me to be baptized,
As the prophets did proclaim.
He is the promised Messiah,
And the world will not be the same.

When I had baptized Jesus,
There in the Jordan River,
The spirit of God descended on Him,
For the world He would deliver.

Then from heaven, God's voice was heard,
With unbelievable ease,
"This is My beloved Son,
In whom I am well pleased."

The beloved Son of God,
Started His mission on that day.
He made a radical change in the world
That was to never go away.

He preached that you must live by faith,
And run the entire race.
And I will save you thru My deity,
And unmerited saving grace.

My Daily Blessings

"Monday's Blessing"

Hab 2:14
For the earth shall be filled with the knowledge
Of the glory of the Lord, as the waters cover the sea.

Our cup runneth over at the majesty of God,
It's pure as a snow white dove.
Just as the seas are great,
Greater is His eternal love.

"Tuesday's Blessing"

Isa 40:31
But they that wait upon the Lord shall renew their strength;
They shall mount up with wings as eagles;
They shall run, and not be weary;
And they shall walk, and not faint.

God said to be patient,
Or you may go wrong.
He will make new your mind ,
And your soul shall be strong.

As you rise at morning,
You'll feel young just like the past.
You will never tire,
When you move oh so fast.
And when you move at a slower pace,
Your strength will be anew full of His Grace.

"Wednesday's Blessing"

Isa 40:8
The grass withereth, the flower fadeth;
But the word of our god shall stand for ever.

Things that bloom in the pasture land,
Are here for only a very short time.
But His word will rise forever,
From this almighty God of mine.

"Thursday's Blessing"

Mic 7:8
Rejoice not against me, o mine enemy.
When I fall, I shall arise;
When I sit in darkness,
The Lord shall be a light unto me.

If you are against, me, celebrate not;
Defeat for you is a must.
Because of the Lord I shall get up each time,
That I go down to the dust.

Protection for me, He has promised.
And keeping it is a must.
God shall shine His light on me,
And will not allow me to be lost at dusk.

"Friday's Blessing"

Isa 26:3
Thou wilt keep Him in perfect peace,
Whose mind is stayed on Thee.

Because I trusteth in Thee,
When the chaos surrounds me, God calms me,
And keeps me at ease.
He keeps me stable in turmoil,
And gives me perfect peace.

"Saturday's Blessing"

1 Th 1:2
We give thanks to God always for you all,
Making mention of you in our prayers.

When I talk with God at the end of the day,
I'll be sure to remember you.
And His blessings He will give,
For praying for you is what I love to do.

"Sunday's Blessing"

John 3:16
For God so loved the world,
That He gave His only begotten Son,
That whosoever believeth in Him should not perish,
But have everlasting life.

God gave His Son to spread peace and grace,
Over the entire earth.
He gives eternal life to those who believe this;
It is a new birth.

His Love
(Ephesians 3:15)

Devotional

Live each day with the love,
That flows from His throne.
Embrace it tightly with thine heart,
Such peace you have never known.

For love is like the tides,
That does openly ebb and flow;
This is God's desire,
And with it we must freely sow.

When we are down and out,
And feeling really low.
Seek His tender love,
And His peace He will sweetly show.

You are not the only one,
That will see this precious change.
His presence will be visible,
To all within your range.

His love flows like a river,
After a fresh, spring day rain.
It flows within and without,
And everyone does gain.

Show His love to everyone,
The bad and the good.
And all will benefit from it,
Just as Jesus said they would.

Let the love of Christ,
By everyone be seen in you.
And they will see Him in everything
That you say and do.

His love is the breath of life,
That we should know and live by.
To see this change in everyone you meet,
Just give His love a try.

Faith
(Hebrews 11)

Devotional

Faith like Grace,
Is a gift from our almighty God.
It is something awakening,
And for this you should never nod.

If you are rich in faith,
You shall always be blessed.
Just believe in Jesus Christ,
And He will do the rest.

Accept this gift of faith,
And hold it with a tight embrace.
After you do this, He will bless you,
With His eternal saving grace.

Faith is oh so spiritual,
And very much divine.
And it is a very special gift,
Of its own kind.

Faith in Christ not only saves,
It combats all of the enemy's sins.
Without faith in Jesus,
A true life you can never begin.

We walk by faith is what Paul did say,
And I know that he is right.
It is our light in the day time,
And also our lamp at night.

When you trust in Christ,
Your soul like an eagle shall soar.
"I forgive thee," He will say,
"Go and sin no more."

The gift of faith to me,
God has so richly and freely given.
Without this faith no one can enter,
Into his wonderful heaven.

Trust in the faith,
That will set you oh so free.
Trust in Christ,
And this you will see.

Accept His gift,
of faith today.
And be saved by grace,
For it is the only way.

My Hope For You

As I complete this book of poems,
Here at this time,
Know they are special to me,
This small token of mine.

I hope that you liked them,
And they helped you to see,
Just what the Lord Jesus,
Really does mean to me.

He said that He is the way, the truth,
And the life today.
If you want to go to the Father,
You must go thru Him He did say.

The words of Jesus is the way,
You should steadily go.
For He is the life,
That we all should already know.

You must be saved by grace thru faith,
Said the Apostle Paul.
Believe in your heart and confess with your mouth,
And you can have it all.

Accept His free gift of grace today,
And you will be so free.
To live in heaven with Him,
For eternity.

Jesus' desire,
Is that all should come to Him.
But for those who refuse,
There is a place for them.

The inspirited scriptures were freely given to us;
They were not for sale.
If we follow what they say,
We will be free of Satan's hell.

So as I close this small poem,
I ask you to come to Jesus today.
Trust in Him and His holy word,
For this is truly the only way.

Jesus the Christ of God, the Messiah,
One day will come for us.
John was told this by Him and the apostle replied,
"Come Lord Jesus."

J. Michael